T0353217

SAMI IBRAHIM

Sami Ibrahim is a writer from London. His play *two Palestinians go dogging* won Theatre Uncut's 2019 Political Playwriting Award and will be produced at the Royal Court in May 2022. His play *Fledgling* was recently broadcast on Radio 4 and his piece *The European Hare* was shortlisted for the Bruntwood Prize 2019. He has been on attachment at the National Theatre Studio and Theatr Clwyd, and is under commission at Headlong, Paines Plough, The Yard and the Almeida. Other theatre credits include *Wonder Winterland* (Oxford School of Drama/Soho Theatre, 2019); *Wind Bit Bitter, Bit Bit Bit Her* (VAULT Festival, 2018); as well as short plays performed at the Sam Wanamaker Playhouse (*Deep Night Dark Night*, 2019/2020); The Bunker (Pint Sized's October Fest, 2018); Southwark Playhouse (Little Pieces of Gold, 2018); The Yard (First Drafts, 2017); and the Brockley Jack (Write Now 7, 2016). For screen, he is currently working on a pilot for Chapter One Pictures, developing treatments with Expanded Media as well as the BFI/Film London, and is a member of BBC Writersroom.

LAURA LOMAS

Laura Lomas's plays include *The Blue Road* (youth companies at Dundee Rep/Derby Theatre/Royal & Derngate/Theatre Royal Plymouth, 2017); *Joanne* (Clean Break/Soho Theatre, 2015); *Bird* (Derby Live/Nottingham Playhouse/UK tour, 2014); *Blister* (Paines Plough/RWCMD/Gate Theatre, 2014); *Open Heart Surgery* (Theatre Uncut/Southwark Playhouse/Traverse Theatre/Soho Theatre); *The Island* (Nottingham Playhouse/Det Norske Oslo, 2009); *Wasteland* (New Perspectives Theatre/Derby Live, 2009). Radio plays include *Fragments* (Afternoon Drama, BBC Radio 4); *My Boy* (Somethin' Else Productions/BBC Radio 4, winner of Best Drama Bronze, Sony Radio Academy Awards 2013); and *Lucy Island* (BBC Radio 3, The Wire). Screen credits include *Hanna* (Amazon); *Glue* (E4), and *Rough Skin* for Coming UP (Channel 4/Touchpaper), which was nominated for Best British Short at the BIFAs and Best UK Short at Raindance Film Festival.

SABRINA MAHFOUZ

Sabrina Mahfouz is a writer and performer, raised in London and Cairo. Sabrina's published and produced theatre work includes *The History of Water in the Middle East* at the Royal Court; *Chef*, a Fringe First Award winner; *Dry Ice*, for which she was nominated in The Stage Awards for Acting Excellence; *With a Little Bit of Luck*, which won Best Drama Production in the BBC Radio & Music Awards; *Clean*, a Herald Angel Award winner, which transferred to New York; and an adaptation of Malorie Blackman's celebrated YA novel *Noughts & Crosses* for Pilot Theatre. She is a Fellow of the Royal Society of Literature (FRSL) and her debut non-fiction book, *These Bodies of Water: Notes on the British Empire, the Middle East and Where We Meet*, will be published in May 2022 by Tinder Press.

Sami Ibrahim
Laura Lomas
Sabrina Mahfouz

METAMORPHOSES

Inspired by Ovid

NICK HERN BOOKS

London
www.nickhernbooks.co.uk

A Nick Hern Book

Metamorphoses first published as a paperback original in Great Britain in 2021 by Nick Hern Books Limited, The Glasshouse, 49a Goldhawk Road, London W12 8QP

Designed and typeset by Nick Hern Books, London
Printed in Great Britain by Mimeo Ltd, Huntingdon, Cambridgeshire PE29 6XX

A CIP catalogue record for this book is available from the British Library

ISBN   978 1 83904 010 8

Woodland
CARBON
www.woodlandcarbon.co.uk
NICK HERN BOOKS
Printed on Carbon Captured paper

Metamorphoses was first performed at the Sam Wanamaker Playhouse, Shakespeare's Globe, London, on 6 October 2021 (previews from 30 September), with the following cast:

STEFFAN DONNELLY
FIONA HAMPTON
CHARLIE JOSEPHINE
IRFAN SHAMJI

Co-Director	Sean Holmes
Co-Director	Holly Race Roughan
Designer	Grace Smart
Candle Consultant	Simeon Miller

Contents

Introduction   9

A Note on Translation – Skin   11

Achilles   13

Actaeon   14

Arachne   20

Caesar   25

Cephalus and Procris   26

The Creation   31

Eurydice   33

Hecuba, Polyxena and Polydorous   34

Io   37

Juno and Jupiter   44

Medea   46

Midas and the Judgement of Apollo   48

The Minotaur, Ariadne, Theseus and Scylla   50

Myrrha   56

Orpheus   59

Orpheus and the Ciconian Women   62

Pentheus and Bacchus   65

Phaethon and Phoebus   67

Philemon and Baucis   73

Procne and Philomela   78

Introduction

This text was written by three writers but was shaped and influenced by two directors, a load of actors, and all the people who were part of our conversations along the way. Each writer was in charge of their own stories but these stories were developed by a whole company throughout workshops and rehearsals. We've decided not to credit individual stories to individual writers so as not to undermine the idea that this was a shared project.

The bulk of the writing was done during the summer of 2020, in the midst of the Covid-19 pandemic. We'd meet over Zoom every couple of weeks to discuss Ovid's stories, and our reactions to them. These conversations were informed by the events of that summer. As the UK and much of the world was in a state of lockdown, as the murder of George Floyd provoked global protests, as government incompetence in the UK led to rising death counts. It felt like a time when the structural inequalities in our societies were being laid bare. When the forces of chaos and power, and their effect on the rest of us, were exposed. The violent, tragic, sometimes humorous and often absurd nature of these events all informed our interpretation of Ovid's stories. We would like to think we have found hope amongst the chaos too.

Because of the nature of the play we want the text to be more of a jumping-off point rather than something that is set in stone. It is an invitation to play and to explore.

The stories are presented here in alphabetical order but, in any future productions, we'd want you to make your own decisions as to the order the stories could go in (as well as which stories to include and exclude).

In some stories, we've clearly marked out who should speak which line, in others we've given a hint of how lines should be shared out, and sometimes we've just written a story as a single block of text. You should feel free to divide up lines however you wish, for as many voices as you wish.

Sami Ibrahim
Laura Lomas
Sabrina Mahfouz

A Note on Translation

Skin

23 mentions of skin
where to begin
begin with a cow
black and white
or brown
Io
a woman turned into a cow.

The Latin word for skin is pellis

or cutis or tergum or corium
or tunica or paellis or tergus
or pellicula or mastruca or
corius or tegmentum or
membrana or tegus or
folliculus or excuviae or
mastruga or paellicula or
scortum or deglubo or decorio

all with other meanings
such as armour or leather
or back or bark or peel or hide
so you begin to see that the beginning
is never that,
translation choosing the end point
but in the end
there are 22 more mentions of skin.
Next most seen in English as
'her native whiteness'
describing Io as she returns to human form.
Latin word for white here is albus,
also meaning bright and clear
so she could have been 'native bright'

meaning
the glow of returning to her original form
after being chased around the world
for decades as a cow, by a mosquito.

Another word for white is candidus,
which also means bright and shining,
brown yellow beige black skin can be
bright and shining,
someone chose for it to not mean this.

Whiteness was decided
where it wasn't
so the translators of the time
could please their prejudice,
ancient texts to prove a racism invented.

The myths themselves came from
Libya, Ethiopia, Turkey, Syria
Greece
let's just always say Greece / Italy
and it will become the end we want
another word for white is increto
which also means chalk –
or whitewash.

Achilles

Achilles. Son of a king and a nymph. Warrior of the Trojan war.

Some say I'm the greatest warrior that ever lived.

Some say I'm a whore son of a bitch.

Both are right.

I cut off a lot of heads

and I did a lot of dodgy sex stuff.

One thing I really regret.

The whole 'sacrifice Polyxena at the foot of my grave' demand.

I was really overwhelmed with the power of being a ghost.

A heroic ghost too, I had the whole Greek army just waiting to do,

well, absolutely whatever I asked them to.

I know it was hard on Hecuba, to lose another daughter,

but it was Polyxena who led me to my death.

Yes, I could have asked for Paris, the man who actually shot me in the heel,

to be sacrificed instead, but I didn't and that's what I'm here to face.

Maybe I thought me and her... who knows.

She managed to escape in one of the tributaries of the River Styx,

so I never got to explore where that thought might go.

I've had a lot of time down here for self-reflection

and I can conclude that this demand was particularly selfish of me.

On a broader level, thinking about my childhood,

I don't think it's advisable to bring someone up to think they're glorious

and celebrate their skills in bringing death and destruction and violence

to everything they touch.

It's just… weird.

And there's not much room left then for, you know, love.

Which is where I'm at in my journey.

Realising that's all it was about, all I wanted, through all the wars.

Too late now of course, but it's always good to work on yourself.

Sorry, Polyxena. Peace.

Actaeon

Actaeon was a nobleman

Son of Aristaeus

Grandchild of the gods

Some say he was the greatest hunter in all of Greece

It's summer

The shadows, short. Midday heat.

Actaeon and his men have been out since first light, they've risen with the dawn and sweated through all the colours of the morning

Their nets are full. Their hands filthy. Their dogs are tired, their claws and their jaws, matted with the blood of dead animals

It's time to go home

We're in the middle of the forest. The bowl of a mountain range surrounds us. The sun bakes and bounces off hard rock, arid earth.

And close by to all this, in the valley of Gargaphia, there is a gorge. Hidden by trees, unknown to the hunters, this mountain well, is the bathing place of

Diana

Goddess of the hunt

And it's hot, did we say it was hot?

Diana is bathing, her hunt done, she stands on the edge of the cool water, her body glistening with fresh blood

And there she undresses

Her nymphs help her

One takes her sword

Another her bow and arrows

Another loosens her thick hair, tousled and knotted from the morning's charge

Another removes her gown

And a final takes her wreathed crown

Until she stands there,

Dappled in forest light

And this goddess is beautiful

This goddess is enormous, full of blood and heat

Her eyes shine

And her body radiates

As into the water she climbs, and sinks, her whole self under, until she emerges, at the foot of the gorge, flooded by water and light, and there she stays, the water cascading over her gigantic body, as her nymphs wash and bathe her

Now Actaeon is walking close by

His blood still racing from the last kill

He's lost his hunting party

He's taken refuge in the high pines and cool earth of the dark forest

When he hears, the gargling of the gorge

And he's pulled, not by curiosity, but by something deeper, something more like fate, towards the sound

And so, he goes through the dappled light

And all the while the sound is moving through his body

He cuts through the trees

The sound becoming louder, he scrambles up a steep bank, the noise now beating in his chest and his head

And a wind rushes down, through the trees to warn him

But still, he goes

Because this sound, is the sound of his own desire, it's the sound of his own blood moving through his own veins

He skids down a mossy scree, his whole body vibrating

Until all at once he reaches a clearing, and there he follows,

The ripples of the water, each rung disappearing as he traces a line to the origin of their energy

And sees

At the foot of the gorge

The Goddess Diana

Naked. In all her beauty

–

The nymphs scream

They twist their demented faces

They scatter to shield the naked goddess

But it's no use

So high is this goddess

So big and so beautiful

She rises up, above them all

And Actaeon, he can't help but stare

As if in seeing her, he is suddenly seeing eternity

As if this moment could sustain him

As if he could feast on it for a thousand years

And somewhere in the depths of his conscience he knows he should turn away

Somewhere he knows, that this isn't right

This sight, it isn't his

This moment, this memory

Because this goddess is divine

She is divine

She is so much more than his mind can hold, she is so much more than his sight will allow

And the nymphs they scream, their shrieks piercing the sky

And Diana she turns her breast away from him

But still, he stares

His heart pounding, body tense, breath gulping

As the force of that water, in his head and in his chest, rips a river right through him

And Diana eyes this king of the hunt

And she watches, as he feasts himself on her body

She sees his hunger and his greed

And her body remembers

A billion others

Other women, in other forms

All of them banquets

Non-consensual feasts

And with that thought comes another

As wooded horns begin to splinter through Actaeon's forehead

As his hands become hoofs,

As his skin melts and turns to fur,

His body buckles,

As she spears an arrow of terror through his spine

And Actaeon bolts

Flees

Through the dense forest, those high pines

His breath short, hooves pounding

He gallops with the heart of the hunted, out out onto that heat-beaten rock

And he calls out

For his men, and for his dogs

But all that comes out is a strange rip, not quite animal, not quite human

And now his dogs are upon him

Hungry, and fierce

They chase

This stag through the sun-crusted landscape, arid earth, damp forest

Till by the river, as Actaeon glimpses sight of his reflection, the first dog takes him

Clamped tight in the vice of his jaw, he drags the muscle from
the bone

And the second dog ascends, ripping hair, piercing flesh

And the third, and the fourth and the fifth

Wet with blood, as Actaeon howls, a noise, not quite human, not
quite animal

He turns to Mount Olympus, and with his eyes he implores
the gods

But they ignore him

As a sixth dog mounts him

And a seventh and an eighth

And his companions, they call out, as they watch the bloody
feast

Their mouths wet with excitement

Actaeon, Actaeon! They shout and curse his absence

Actaeon! Actaeon!

And they watch, their blood pulsing

And each time they call, the stag's head arches

But they do not realise

They cannot see

And Diana, she watches

From the top of the mountain

Actaeon's legs twitch and his body convulse, as there on the
beaten rock, his own dogs consume him

Arachne

Um. Hi. My name is Arachne. I come from Turkey.

I am a spider. But I wasn't always. We all change.

I'm telling my story today for the sake of art.

The sake of truth. The sake of change. All one and the same.

My mum died when I was a kid.

I got married young.

Didn't get to travel, I wasn't ever really interested in it.

I was arrogant in a lot of ways back then,

I truly believed my mind's eye could see whatever landscape,

whatever city splendours it wanted to without having to move from my loom.

I was – I still am – a weaver. I got famous for it.

As much as a village girl can get famous

without much leaving her house.

I'd felt it in my fingers since I was a kid.

The pictures, the colours, they were just there,

pulsating to be let out and made into woollen wonders.

But I had to work at it to get where I did.

Hours I spent exercising my thumb so it could turn a spindle better,

testing my eyes for days on grains of sand

so I could stand to thread needles in seconds,

years of absorbing every shade of every colour to my memory

so I'd never need to find the thing I wanted to depict,

not even a painting of it.

Not the kind of things that get you many friends.

I didn't mind, I'd gladly chosen my art.

So it pissed me off when people said,

'oh you must be the pupil of Minerva,

that great goddess of art and craft and strategy?'

I'd say

'no, actually, no god has ever stepped their precious foot in my home.

I learnt this alone. No help is given to girls like me except from their own selves.'

Well. This did not go down well at all.

Everyone would beg me to credit Minerva with at least a little help.

A skill like mine couldn't just be hard work and human-given art.

I would anger the gods.

I didn't give a shit.

Life had been tough and I was hard enough to take on a god.

Let her come, I said.

A little old lady was the last who came begging me to praise Minerva

for her supposed gift to me.

She could see in my eyes only her age saved her from my slap,

which I put into words instead of my hands

as I started telling her about herself,

how such an old woman should be more concerned with her own family

than coming to tell me, a stranger, what I should do

and anyway

'I've already told Minerva if she has a problem with it,

let's settle it.'

Shit. The old woman was actually Minerva in disguise wasn't
she?

Yep. And hell-bent young Arachne didn't back down, not for
a second.

We were to go head to head on a tapestry,

for all to judge who was the most skilled.

I warped and wefted like my life depended on it.

Cos, well, as you've likely guessed due to me now being a spider,
it did.

I did my finest work.

Each colour curved into my mind until it became another

and that transferred perfectly onto the wool,

magical blending of life's glow

and yes, hers was pretty good too.

But where the difference really showed

was in the stories that we both told.

Minerva's tapestry was gods galore,

their golden egos and thrones,

crowning herself in her own art.

I knew that if I depicted her and the other gods

in the gleam of my thread with regal heads

and righteous tridents,

the way they give us sun

and rain and sheep and trees

and even if they are sometimes mean

it is for the good of us, to learn, to grow,

I knew if I did this then I would not only save my life,

but likely be given some kind of prize.

It would have been nice for me and my husband, and I loved him.

But it would have been a lie.

I tore off their crowns.

I threaded the blood they brought to every patch of ground

where they raped and raped and raped and raped

and I sewed every moment of those moments as horror

and murder and I curdled their 'enticed' and 'disguised'

and 'convinced' and 'deceived' and 'hoodwinked' and 'fooled'

and 'baited' and 'begetted' and my fingertips bled

and my work was a mirror to the gods

and Minerva ripped every piece of it to shreds.

Then, in the snowfall of my masterpiece

she took my weaving shuttle

and she whacked me over the head with it

again again again again

too much for me, the strength of a god,

I admitted it, but still wouldn't let her kill me.

Avoiding a fifth and final blow

I found a rope, tied it round my neck

quickly stood on a stool by a beam

knotted the rope end round it

kicked the stool and choked.

Minerva came and lifted my knees.

I was forced to breathe.

Pity, she said she felt,

but I knew it was her fear of truth.

She couldn't let me win.

If I died by my own hand after what I'd weaved

it would make the honesty of it hang proud forever,

even if she destroyed every last stitch of it,

so she sprinkled some venomous herbs over me

and my entire body sank through the noose

to become this, a spider,

to weave always without threat,

to let the god's story shine unhindered

in this world and the next.

Caesar

I am Augustus, first ever emperor of Rome,

I am bringer of peace and harmony

over all our lands and people.

A coloniser such as me

could never be plain and simple mortal flesh.

I have blessed humanity.

And in doing so, I rise above the species I bless.

So…

I transformed my adopted dad, Caesar,

into a god, so I would necessarily be a half-god.

I did it with the power of power.

It was also done after he died,

so the timing worked well.

If it wasn't for me,

people would remember him as a dictator,

a great military Roman commander, sure,

but who cares when it all ends by being stabbed

twenty-three times by sixty of your own men,

and especially by your greatest friend, Brutus,

in a ridiculous attempt to take power.

This is the tragedy he, and I,

would be memorialised by.

And I wanted people to worship him, not cry for him.

So the deification made perfect sense.

Cities often make its people feel like

they could be a god within it.

Of course they can't.

They really, really cannot

be a god in their own city.

Unless, of course, they are me.

Cephalus and Procris

A spear hovers in front of PROCRIS.

PROCRIS. There is my husband Cephalus.

Blue eyes.

Toned legs.

Small brain.

One day, he decides – on a whim – to test how faithful I am.

No evidence, he just has a small brain.

But still, he puts on a disguise to conduct his experiment.

It is not a very good disguise.

But he thinks it's good.

He approaches me in a forest.

He starts flirting with me.

He thinks if I flirt back then it means I am an unfaithful wife.

I think that it's some kind of role-play game, or maybe he's just lost it because of the heat, but either way I play along.

You know.

OOOH, HELLO HANDSOME STRANGER, LOOK AT
THOSE BEAUTIFUL BLUE EYES THAT LOOK
NOTHING LIKE MY HUSBAND'S.

And then he… well he overreacts a bit.

He says.

Shame on you, foul traitress.

It is I, your husband.

Which was obvious, but still he is insistent.

And mine eyes do convict you of perfidy!

Well what can you say to that?

I'm very unimpressed.

He keeps shouting.

I tell him to piss off.

He tells me to fuck off.

And I do.

I go to the woods.

I call his bluff.

I join a commune.

Women-only.

And then – of course – he gets jealous.

He decides he wants me back.

I decide he should apologise.

Which he does – be fair to him – he apologises, on his knees,
with a lot of crying and snot and begging and pleading.

It is embarrassing.

But I have a soft spot for him.

I leave the commune, I go home.

And I give my husband a gift.

Something I receive while I am out in the woods, an object that is precious to me, that I want him to have.

As a symbol of our coming-together.

That object happens to be a spear.

This spear.

He hunts with it.

Hunts down beasts, animals – gets his hound to attack them.

One day his hound is turned to marble – in front of his eyes – as she bites into the neck of a fleeing animal.

These things happen, he tells me.

Another day, in between hunting, he rests under a tree.

As he rests, he calls out.

And I know what he says, because one of my servants overhears him calling out.

Come, Aura.

Soothe me, in this putrid heat.

Aura.

And the servant tells me, that very evening, what she's heard.

She says that my husband was calling out to another woman.

A woman called Aura.

Which is curious.

Because I trust my husband.

Because we are stuck in this strained marriage because he accused me and now to find out that it is actually him that is…

–

So the next day I follow my husband.

I watch him as he hunts.

I watch him as he rests.

I feel the sun's heat tighten around my body

And then I hear him.

–

Aura.

–

There it is: a simple word.

And I believe he is being unfaithful.

It clouds my senses.

That this woman is the one he calls out to, that she is so, so available to him that he just has to call out her name and

And I let out a gasp.

A stumble.

Leaves rustle.

Twigs crack.

He hears the sound.

I see him.

He thinks he hears an animal.

His ears detect it.

Pricking up.

Muscles on edge.

Sharp and quick.

Standing.

I step back.

He steps forward.

And he throws his spear and it

Gliding.

In the air.

I watch it hover.

Like it has always hovered.

Sharp, aimed at me.

Like it has always been trained at me.

Since the day I met this man, this spear has pointed at my stomach, itching and impatient and waiting for the single moment when it

The spear wedges into PROCRIS*'s stomach and she collapses.*

CEPHALUS *takes over.*

CEPHALUS. is let loose.

From my hand.

And strikes her.

And the last thing she does is whisper.

Do not marry her.

Do not marry this woman called Aura.

I try to explain that Aura is nothing, no one.

Aura is the spirit of the wind, sent to cool hunters on a hot day.

Aura is emptiness.

But a breeze rushes through the trees and the words are whipped away.

And I try repeating myself but her brain has switched off.

So quick.

The breeze still blows.

I look up to the sky.

And, just beyond the clouds, I see the gods are laughing.

The Creation

We are here to make sense of it all.

How everything transforms and we start again.

–

Before the world begins, it is dark for a long time.

Like this.

It is a raw and lifeless bulk – nothing else.

An undigested mess.

But out of this, a world has to be summoned.

The first things the gods do is sever the sky and the sea from the land.

They rip the elements apart and twist them round into an orb – they create this planet.

They create order.

The sea is poured out over the earth.

The land is stretched into flat plains.

But, still, we're missing things.

Up in the stratosphere, the gods organise: they sort the wind from the rain, they send the cold up into the north, they send the heat down south.

Where the sea overflows, the gods let it drip into rivers and streams.

And where there is too much land – like overflowing pastry – they bunch it up: they form hills and mountains.

The gods carve out canyons and valleys with a chisel.

Except it is still dark

And the gods are keen to see what their creation looks like, so they add light to the mix.

A sun.

The sun rises.

It's nailed into place and burns in the sky.

The only thing needed now is life.

Plants sprouting out of the earth.

Fish filling the seas.

Life is added to every corner of this planet.

Proudly, the gods sprinkle it on.

They crack each animal's bones into place as it steps onto four legs.

Then they create humans.

The gods mould humans out of crude dirt.

They give some humans wisdom, other humans violence.

And these humans are wobbly, at first, on their two little legs.

But they are able to step forward.

The other creatures on this planet, they look down, but the humans, they look up.

They seem promising.

Eurydice

I've died twice

The first time was on my wedding day

I married an artist. A singer. His name was Orpheus, he played the lyre. You might have heard of him?

The wedding was nice. Great food. Lots of people, big cake

But after the ceremony, I went for a walk. Bare feet, long grass and I stood on a snake. A viper. She turned and bit me. I died

The Ferryman carried me across the River Styx to the underworld, where I stayed

I hated it at first. Fucking cold. And damp.

But after a while it wasn't so bad. Pluto's alright. Persephone's a good laugh.

One day my husband, Orpheus arrives. Still with blood in his body, very much alive and he decides that he's got to make this big show about getting me back

He begs them. On his hands and knees. It's embarrassing. He's all 'please please, give her back, I'll do anything'.

And then he starts singing.

A song.

And this song is so annoying that in the end Pluto and Persephone are just like 'take her, go'

But they put this condition on it. They say that I'm to follow him, on that path that leads up to the living. But he can't look at me. Not even once. He's not allowed to turn back

And so we go. It's a steep journey, Orpheus complains a lot. Each time he asks me if I'm there, I reply 'Yes. I am here. I'm right here'

About halfway up, Orpheus gets a stitch and we have to stop for twenty minutes. Him looking one way. Me staring at the back of his head.

We carry on. It gets dark. Orpheus gets scared. He starts calling out to me. He says 'Euridyce, I'm scared.' He can't hear my footsteps. A soul is lighter than a body. He begins to cry

He gets himself in a right state

I try to comfort him, but he can't hear me over his sobs and nearing the top he turns

but it's too late. The moment he sees me, I'm already gone.

This is how I die the second time

The spirits take me, my body evaporates

And here I wait. For eternity. Eurydice.

Hecuba, Polyxena and Polydorous

This is the story from my perspective.

I am Hecuba

My son is Polydorous.

My husband sends our son away from Troy – for safety – to live with a king.

Not long after, Troy falls.

We are defeated.

And this king, in charge of my son, hears the news.

He takes my son's gold.

He stabs my son.

He throws him off a cliff.

One child killed.

In some far-off land.

So far-off that I don't discover his death for years.

In the meantime, this is how the second one goes.

As my city is ransacked, soldiers arrive.

They are accompanied by the ghost of Achilles.

Achilles demands the sacrifice of a young girl in his honour.

He makes a demand.

A *ghost* makes a demand.

And no one questions this.

He points to Polyxena.

Polyxena is my daughter.

She goes bravely, she is unflinching.

And the executioner drives the knife into her chest with a single, sharp movement.

After is it done, I lift her up.

I clean her blood-clotted hair.

I place her in the earth.

And I turn to the gods – I ask them

What reason is there for me to live, except to attend the funerals of my children?

The gods shrug.

–

–

–

–

One day, I go for a walk on the beach.

I see a speck on the horizon.

A blob of flesh.

Flashes of red oozing out of it.

And then it arrives at my feet.

Placed there, with a chuckle, by the gods.

It is the body of my son – knife wounds dug into his torso.

I am not angry.

I decide that justice comes when I confront my son's murderer.

I travel across the sea.

I pretend that I have gold to offer the king and he agrees to meet me.

I dig my fingers into his eyes.

I pull out his eyeballs.

Filthy with blood.

I rip his eye sockets from his skull.

I crush his skull.

The man is dead.

And it is no more than what he did to my son.

This is what I try to explain.

And yet, when the king's subjects see what I have done, they don't listen.

The king's subjects attack me.

First they call me mad, then they hurl stones, they are a mob, they are howling and snarling.

And I defend myself.

Now I am angry.

I charge at them.

I shout at them,

attack them

with

with a growl

with a fury

with all my

and I am screaming

and I am

I am

screaming

and

snarling

and

and

Her voice turns into a bark.

It keeps barking.

Helpless.

She transforms into a dog.

Io

Io lived with her father, near a stream.

She collected water from this stream every day.

One morning she was stopped by a stranger.

Not a stranger: a god: the king of the gods, in fact: Jupiter.

He came up to her and he winked.

He watched as she collected water.

He talked about all the dangerous men who like to take advantage of vulnerable young women – like her.

He held out his hand and told her to come with him.

But Io ran.

And Jupiter ran after her.

And when he got bored of this chase, he called out to the heavens.

He drew clouds over from the west, he let a fog descend from the north.

The sun was blotted out as Jupiter enveloped the land in darkness.

Io held her hand in front of her face but couldn't make it out.

Then she felt the footsteps of a god.

Vibrating the earth.

Jupiter tracked her down.

He raped her.

–

Up in the heavens, Juno noticed this darkness.

She was the wife of Jupiter.

She knew him – she knew the things that he did – and she knew that these very specific weather patterns were a sign of something suspicious.

So Juno stepped onto our planet.

She waved her hand, the clouds disappeared and she called out to her husband.

And Jupiter heard his wife calling – he knew she was coming.

So he did the only the thing he could think of: he turned Io into a cow.

And when Juno arrived, Jupiter simply stood there.

Next to this cow.

Maybe he rested an elbow on her, tried to look casual.

Innocent.

Yes?

And Juno was hardly convinced but she played along.

Where did this beautiful cow come from, husband?

From the earth. She emerged from the earth.

And Juno seized on this.

She?

It.

He corrected himself. Juno watched him.

Do you think it might be a gift for me, husband, this very beautiful cow that emerged from the earth?

Jupiter didn't respond.

He could see the mistrusting glint in Juno's eye.

He weighed it up in his head – saying *yes*, saying *no*.

And, in the end, he relented: he gave Juno the cow.

Juno placed her hands on Io.

She stared into Io's eyes.

Io tried to tell Juno what had happened but no human words could form.

Not when her tongue was so swollen and uncomfortable in this strange body.

The only sound that emerged was a soft moo.

–

Juno couldn't find any answers so she placed the cow under safe keeping.

She gave Io to Argus – who had a hundred eyes.

Who could look in any direction, but always kept one eye on Io.

Who might fall asleep with ninety-nine eyes shut, but always remained awake with the hundredth.

Argus made Io plough his field.

He locked her in a stable at night.

Some days, he let her out to graze. And every time he did, Io would wander back to the stream near her father's house.

She would wait by the stream, listening out for her father's footsteps.

It was a long wait.

When their paths did finally cross, all Io's father saw was a cow.

A lovely cow – but just a cow.

And this cow was acting strangely.

The cow followed him.

Io's father sped up.

Io sped up.

And she nudged him, with her soft, wet nose.

He stopped.

He looked at the cow.

The cow licked his hand – and then pushed him.

Gently – because he was old.

To the riverbank.

There, in the mud, with her hoof, she drew

An I

And an O.

–

And Io's father knew.

But he did nothing.

What could he do?

And Io could do nothing.

–

Before they knew it, Argus had taken Io back.

He took her away, up, to the peak of a mountain, where his eyes kept constant watch.

Meanwhile, Io's father prayed to the gods.

Jupiter heard him.

Now the gods don't normally bother with human emotions. And it's true, Jupiter wasn't exactly burdened by the weight of Io and her father's grief.

Still, in all his benevolence (and because he had an afternoon going spare), the ruler of the gods decided to set Io free.

He sent Mercury.

He's the messenger of the gods – with stories stored in his back pocket.

Mercury arrived on the mountaintop with a smile.

As Argus prepared a simple meal for his guest, Mercury turned to Io and winked at her.

Then he took out a bottle of wine and handed it to Argus.

Argus drank – and drank – as Mercury told him stories.

All different kinds of stories: long ones, convoluted ones, stories like this one.

Meandering and strange, full of adjectives and nouns and gods and adverbs and very slowly... Argus drifted off to sleep.

Only a few eyes at first, creeping shut, as the stories shifted and twisted.

And then more eyes.

Each one prompting the next. Like a ripple. When Argus was finally asleep, when the last eye had shut, when Mercury had checked and double-checked, he took out a knife.

He looked at Io.

Then he stabbed every single one of Argus's eyes.

He cut off Argus's head.

Threw it down the side of the mountain.

–

When he was done, Mercury turned to Io.

His clothes flecked with blood, he held out his hand and told her

Jupiter sent me to set you free.

–

Up in the heavens, Juno was furious.

She saw what had happened and understood what Jupiter had done.

She summoned a Fury.

She sent this Fury to infect Io with a kind of terror.

This terror made Io run.

Before Mercury could catch her, before Jupiter could stop her, Io ran.

With a Fury stamping up and down in her head, Io ran and ran, heading back to the stream by her home.

Jupiter watched Io as she fled across continents.

Then he went to Juno, while she was collecting Argus's eyes, and he begged her to pity Io.

He said he felt remorse.

But Juno ignored him.

Instead, very precisely, Juno picked up each and every one of Argus's eyes. They had calcified – like sparkling jewels – and she placed them onto the plumage of a bird. The first peacock, whose feathers spread out with a flourish.

Then, when she was done, she smiled this wary smile.

She looked across the earth.

She saw Io, foaming and mad – she saw Io's father weeping.

And then she turned to Jupiter.

She shrugged.

Set her free.

As Io stood, looking at her strange reflection in the stream, she became human again.

–

Of course, Jupiter made all sorts of promises.

He said he was done with his old ways, he promised it.

And Io finally went home.

She hugged her father.

She tried to explain what had happened but the words wouldn't form.

She settled back into a silent life.

She fetched water from the stream.

She watched her father die.

She buried him.

She had a child.

A son – Jupiter's son, to be precise – and she raised him, by herself.

He grew up and they spent many happy years together.

Except, even now, when she sits opposite him, when they share a meal, when her son asks who his father is, when he asks for the stories of his mother's life – when he asks for *this* story – her jaw locks up.

Her tongue suddenly becomes swollen and uncomfortable.

And she gets this feeling: that whenever she speaks, the only sound to emerge will be a garbled moo.

And so she doesn't.

Juno and Jupiter

JUPITER. What great love story doesn't have a fierce
    disagreement at the heart of it?
    This one is no different.

JUNO. Except it is between the king and queen of the gods
    and they had to put up with each other for all of eternity,
    really.

JUPITER. Juno and Jupiter had a lot of issues, but on most of
    them they reached an agreement of some sort.
    However, there was one area which the years hadn't solved.
    Juno felt there was a bit more take from Jupiter during their
    love-making.

JUNO. It was all about him – when he finished, it was finished
    and she was, understandably, not a fan of this time frame.

JUPITER. He didn't quite see it her way,
    He thought she wanted more
    than any other woman had ever asked him for.

JUNO. Juno pointed out that most women had not asked him
    at all.
    Nor had he asked them.

JUPITER. *Everyone knows a woman gets more out of sex than
    a man.*

JUNO. Juno wanted to boil his eyes in oil at this moment.

    *Who is this everyone, then? I'd love to meet them. I mean,
    I can pretty much guarantee it won't be a woman saying
    women get more out of sex than men.*

JUPITER. Jupiter decided it was time to call Tiresias.

    A NARRATOR *appears.*

NARRATOR. A quick footnote on Tiresias: He's a man. He
    used to be a woman. He was a man before that.

    He stumbled across some snakes.

They were having sex. In the undergrowth. And Tiresias picked up a stick and prodded the snakes and he was transformed into a woman.

He spent seven years as a woman – fell in love, married a beautiful man, fucked him – a lot – and had children with him and they were beautiful.

One day he returned to the snakes.

He picked up a stick, he prodded them again, he was transformed into a man.

JUNO. *So there you go. Answered. If he thought sex was so great as a woman WHY would he start fighting snakes to get transformed back into a man?*

JUPITER. Jupiter ordered Mercury to bring Tiresias to them ASAP.

JUNO. Too tired for sex but not too tired to wait to be right, who knows how long.

JUPITER. Mercury has wings, he's back already.
Tiresias, I've heard your story and I want a simple answer. Is sex more pleasurable for a man or a woman?

Pick an audience member and wait for them to answer the question. Keep asking the question until they give the answer 'woman'.

JUNO. *Of course. Tiresias is called here by the big manly king god and he says what he wants to hear. Wondering what wonders will be bestowed upon him by the infamous Jupiter. Trying to make it so that I, a queen god, have to feel grateful for sex! You think I'll fall for that? I see you, Tiresias. I see you so clearly I'm gonna make sure you never see a thing again – BAH!*

JUPITER. *Juno! He's blind! Undo what you just did, you psycho!*

Jupiter comforted Tiresias, a fellow man, blinded by a woman's wrath.

He couldn't reverse her terrible deed, but he would make Tiresias see in another way.

A seer, a prophet, beloved by kings and gods.

Tiresias the Great.

Tiresias the Prophet.

JUNO. Oh fuck off!

Medea

You know that feeling when your husband's uncle tries to steal your husband's throne? And your husband, for some reason, refuses to take revenge so the only thing you can do is leave your husband, travel across the wide sea and hunt down this uncle?

Exactly.

I'm Medea, my husband is Jason, this uncle is called Pelias.

I'm a witch.

My favourite power is the one where I make people young again.

I do this by draining that person's blood and replacing it with an elixir.

I hate to brag but it's very effective.

I visit Pelias.

I pretend that Jason has sent me into exile.

I gain Pelias's sympathy.

And one night, around the fire, I tell Pelias about my powers.

I promise that I can make him young.

Now: Pelias is greedy, he feels death hanging above him.

It doesn't take long before he agrees to be transformed.

I tell him to go to bed as normal and, during the night, I'll visit him and perform the operation – in the morning he'll be good as new.

I get Pelias's daughters involved as well.

At midnight, I hand them daggers and I tell them:

Slit the old man's throat, drain his blood.

I point to where they should begin.

Near an artery.

Pelias bleeds quickly.

He wakes – red liquid gushing out of his neck.

He looks up, he sees his daughters, sees the knives they hold.

And before his daughters have a chance to explain, before anything can happen, I snap the old man's windpipe, chop off his head.

He believes his daughters have murdered him.

It is his absolute last thought, I see it in his eyes.

And it is so clever.

And they are so sad.

–

I return home to Jason.

I tell him what I've done for him.

How I thought of him, his soft face, his red lips, as I gripped his uncle's throat.

Love is a series of tasks we perform to prove that we are, in fact, in love.

But Jason

–

You know that feeling when you've murdered your husband's uncle but your husband doesn't appreciate it? And instead of welcoming you home after all these years, he tells you to fuck off and you ask him why and then you find out he's remarried?

–

So I ask to see the children.

Two of them.

And they look just like Jason.

They're gorgeous.

They barely recognise me.

And I take my hands and wrap them round their brittle throats.

The older one first, then the younger.

I remove their breath and leave without saying goodbye.

Midas and the Judgement of Apollo

APOLLO, *playing guitar.*

When the mighty Apollo plays, all believe he is the best in the land.

–

It's clear to see why.

And everyone agrees, by the way.

So many people come up to me, they praise me and love me and they are so kind to me.

–

Except for Midas.

Contrary Midas.

Ignorant Midas.

Tone-deaf Midas.

Dull-witted Midas.

Selfish, boring, music-hating, thick-as-a-brick-wall Midas.

The same Midas who, by the way, once wished for everything he touched to be turned to gold.

Did you hear that?

And then he almost starved.

And he's criticising me?

It's funny.

No, it makes me laugh, it really does.

He is a childish man.

–

I hate Midas!

I hate Midas and I hate people like him who criticise my music when they clearly lack their own technical ability!

–

I give him the ears of a donkey.

And Midas, he tries to hide them.

He wears a hat.

But it is an ugly hat that doesn't suit him.

It's not as good as my hat.

And he can't hide the secret of his ears forever. Someone has to cut Midas's hair.

A servant.

And this servant gets to see Midas's ears.

Hidden under the hat.

At first, the servant is too scared to tell anyone, but he's also too excited to tell no one.

So he digs a hole in the ground.

He whispers the secret of Midas's donkey ears into the hole.

He buries the secret.

–

Soon, out of that same earth, reeds begin to grow.

The secret grows through their stems.

The secret pushes up to the reeds' bushy heads.

And as a soft southern wind blows, the secret is released across the land.

The secret of Midas's donkey ears is no longer a secret.

–

Can you guess who sent that soft southern wind?

No? Maybe?

Let's just say, no one now disputes the fact that I am the best in the land.

The Minotaur, Ariadne, Theseus and Scylla

I grew up watching the men I loved at war.

Most of us daughters of kings did.

Forbidden from battle but wanting it as much –

even more – than they did I think,

us sweet girls were able only to delve

into the gorgeous gore as a lovely eyed spectator.

I ensured my lovely eyes had the best spot,

watching from the top of a tower

built tall by my father to protect him, his kingdom.

Ironically, it is here where his downfall begins.

My heart sang seeing his enemy King Minos

as they fought on the land below the tower's window.

It was love, I couldn't fight it, I needed him inside me,

his beard between my fingers.

For our love, I'd betray my father.

Minos would adore me, Scylla,

the woman who gave herself as a hostage

to stop the bloodshed of thousands, a heroine!

Yes, I knew he was married,

but everyone knew that his weirdo wife

cheated on him with a bull, giving birth to a beast

that Minos, with his understanding heart, allowed her to keep.

His own mum Europa got raped by Apollo

– pretending to be a bull supposedly –

and that's how he, the gorgeous godly Minos, was born,

so maybe that's why he felt some kindness towards such horror.

Whatever the reason, I thought it reasonable that he now got
a treat,

me, his own personal whore willing to sacrifice and serve.

I, Scylla, will end this war.

And for better or for worse, so I did.

Clipping my father's hair as he slept,

handing it to the hands of my love,

Minos – take this lock of hair as if it is the head

of my father, your enemy, you have me, you have victory.

I wait, trembling at being so close to this love of mine.

Imagining his hand reaching to touch my face,

to swear his undying devotion to such a brave woman,

Scylla, forever.

But he hangs his head away from me,

flays his arm out to keep me distant,

disgusted at my love, my sacrifice, my offering.

Sinner! He hurls his sweet chin at me to spit, not kiss.

I call on the gods to fling you away from land and sea!

Disgrace of a woman,

no monster such as you will ever come to Crete!

He leaves. Angry, obviously. And I'm a state.

Praying all the prayers to all the gods,

nodding and rocking like a disgraced woman must.

Then I'm angry in return. My own hair in my hands now.

Shouting at Minos and his fleet of ships,

my sin wasn't such a sin that you couldn't let it win you a war!

Turn your back on me, but not on the victory I gave you!?

Coward, born not of a god in disguise but of a plain old bull

that your mum liked the look of, you took after her savagery,

you deserve a wife who loves a bit of bestiality,

you deserve a bastard Minotaur son to run you into the ground,

your wife would rather fuck a bull than you

and yet you think you can punish me!?

The words, the truth of them, the power in that truth,

the most powerful force I've ever felt,

thrust me into the waves,

gave me the energy to catch his ship

and I clinged, singing my rage to the wet wind,

until it was too much, too fast, too cold,

I felt a beak tear at my legs,

the eyes of an osprey behind me,

eyes that I knew were my father's,

his disbelief at his daughter's betrayal

giving him feathers and flight

and I fell

fell

but did not land.

Wings where my own clinging arms had been sprung up

and in the reflection of the surf I saw myself,

a ciris bird, the word that means 'to cut'.

I loved my new life in the skies.

I never saw an osprey again.

My small, bright body bursting with song.

I kept a nest in Crete, proving Minos wrong once again.

My words must have hurt his pride after all,

as on his return he sacrificed the many bulls he owned,

one hundred of them, blood baths to Jove

and then he goes to Daedalus, asks him to construct a maze,

one that could only bring intricate uncertainty,

and into it he placed his wife's Minotaur son.

It was done.

I was well into my grandmother-hen years

when Theseus came from Athens

and killed the poor imprisoned monster,

in order to save Athenians from being sacrificed to it every nine years,

as part of some strange deal done to avenge the death of Minos's son.

How did Theseus do it though?

Not alone, obviously.

But with a young woman so in love

she'd sacrifice her own family.

History really does just go on and on repeating itself.

Ariadne gave him a magic thread,

so he could do what nobody had ever done –

safely get out of the maze that had long been her brother's jail.

For his victory, she'd ensured no home existed for her in Crete,

so with the Minotaur defeated,

he took her with him on the ship back to Athens.

So far, so slightly better than the way her father treated me.

They stopped at the island of Naxos, for a sleep on dry land, supposedly.

But then, in a move more cowardly than I'd ever seen,

Theseus abandoned Ariadne on the shore as she was sleeping,

the ships leaving before light arrived.

When she woke up she screamed stones to salt.

I wished I could carry more than worms to her,

I flew back and forth to try and distract her with my colours.

She couldn't see me through her tears.

But she could see Bacchus when he arrived in his piercing light,

because when does a god see a young girl upset

and not come and take advantage?

I'm not sure exactly what happened,

my eyes are small and it got dark.

But before long, she was smiling.

Bacchus took Ariadne's crown

and threw it up into the sky –

she was always to shine down upon us now,

a constellation, the corona borealis.

It felt like the right time for me to make my final nest,

looking up at the crest of stars

that speaks of weak men

and the dazzlingly stupid women who help them.

Myrrha

MYRRHA. I wasn't always a tree. I used to be a woman.

I was beautiful. The fairest in all of Panchaia. I had suitors, men from all over the world, who came to beg for my hand, or my bed.

I didn't even look at them. I had desire in my heart for only one man, and so bright did that fire burn

But... I couldn't have him

And so, sick with grief, one night I take my bedsheet and I tie it in a noose to hang from my bedpost.

I'm standing with the knot around my neck when...

My nurse walks in

Beat.

She screams, drags me down

She pleads with me to tell her my troubles

I can't

She implores me, begs, threatens to tell my father

And I can't have that, I can't. I won't and so I say

'God envy my mother, blessed in her husband'

Beat.

And so now it's out

I'm in love with my father

But the nurse is kind. She doesn't judge. She waits till the festival of Ceres, that time when women refuse the love of their men for nine days and nine nights

My father's bed is empty, and as the festivities rage

The nurse goes to him and tells him, there is a girl who desires you

When my father asks 'Who?'

The nurse tells him a servant.

When he enquires as to the age of this girl?

She says 'The same age as your daughter'

That night the nurse leads me, through the pitch-black darkness to my father's chamber.

Three times I stumble, three times I hear an owl screech and I know this to be an omen

But I am boldened, hidden by night.

She leads me to his room.

It's dark.

He can't see me

At the doorway I falter, I want to turn, but the nurse she holds me.

At the foot of his bed, she says

'She is yours'

And so it is

For nine nights, whilst the festival of Ceres rages. We make the world a new. My body changes. And with each breath I transform. My heart stretches, my chest swells, an ocean turns inside me. I lift my head to the ceiling and the walls come away. The sky expands, the night is ripped open and I am here, with all this – new constellations, new colours, new languages

Until…

On the final night, my father brings a candle, determined to see the face of his mistress

Silence.

It's terrible

More silence.

He stands, reaches for his sword

And at this I run

I flee. For nine months across scorched earth, a baby in my belly

When I reach Sabaea, I can't go on

I'm tired, my body aches, swollen with the life inside me

I call out to the gods. I tell them to

'Punish me. I deserve it'

I tell them my life offends the living and my death offends the dead

I say 'Refuse my flesh both life and death'

ADONIS *enters.*

ADONIS. And as she speaks her feet become trees rooted in the earth

Her blood cools and turns to sap

Her body twists, and moans and splinters and the baby in her, it...

Grows

Safe in the belly of a trunk

Until at once, when the time is right, the tree bends, breaks, and out falls the body of a boy

Days turn into years and the child grows

More lean and handsome than any prince

From the bed of his mother and grandfather

Comes this man

They call him Adonis

Orpheus

ORPHEUS *enters singing*.

Imagine a man
Lean-bodied
Dark-eyed
Smooth skin
Bared chest
Very handsome
Are you imagining him?

ORPHEUS *gestures to himself*.

Now imagine this man
Plays an instrument
The most beautiful of all instruments
The lyre
He sings

ORPHEUS *sings*.

And when people hear his voice they rejoice, because it is the
most beautiful sound in all of Greece
Nature opens itself to him
The seas calm, the trees bend, the wind stills

Now imagine this man takes a lover
A beautiful woman
The most beautiful in all of Pierra
Kind eyes
A soulful face
Her name is Eurydice and this man
He is Orpheus

It's their wedding day
Everyone there
The gods
The Graces
Hymen, god of marriage
A great feast, much wine

Shortly after the ceremony my wife goes walking in the long grass, and she steps on a snake, a viper, which turns and sinks its venomous fangs into her bare ankle and kills her
She dies

When I find her I…

ORPHEUS *is distraught.*

I…

I…

I… I… I… take my lyre and I open my throat and I bellow out my sorrow to the high heavens but it's not enough

It's not enough.

It's not…

I rip off my shirt and I beat my bare chest and I clutch at the earth but it's not enough it's not…

So here's what I do. I take my lyre and I go, I descend the long steps to the Taenarian Gate and there, on the shores of the Styx, I summon the Ferryman and demand him to carry me across to the bowels of the underworld and the seat of Haemon

ORPHEUS *looks at the audience.*

It's quite scary

There's a lot of ghosts

I can feel their eyes on me

But I am very brave

I look back at them

ORPHEUS *stares back at the audience. This can last as long as you like.*

Eventually I find Persephone and Pluto and I command them to give me back my wife, I say

GIVE ME BACK MY WIFE!

I take out my lyre and I sing to them

ORPHEUS *sings.*

And my song is so beautiful

It's so beautiful

It is the best song they have ever heard, and it pierces their ice-cold hearts and warms up their blood. It brings tears of sorrow to their dead eyes

Eventually I get them to agree to give me back my wife

But there's a catch

They're sneaky like that the gods

They tell me I can go, ascend the long path to the world of the living, and Eurydice, my love, will follow me, the whole way, she'll be just behind, and when we reach that summit, we'll be reunited.

The only condition

Is that I don't look back

Not once

I don't look back

I say 'Okay fine' and so we go. Eurydice and I. We ascend the steps. I call out, and I hear her voice a faint whisper and I say 'Are you there my love' and she says 'I am here' and all the time I listen for her footsteps, which become fainter and fainter, but still we press forward, and just as we're a few steps from the precipice, a cold thought freezes my brain and I think 'what if they've tricked me', and
so
I
turn
my head
just a little, but in that same instance she's taken, dragged, gasping from me, and disappears, screaming into the abyss of hell

It's not my fault

It wasn't

It was the gods. They tricked me!

ORPHEUS *takes his lyre and leaves*.

Orpheus and the Ciconian Women

Okay so there's this guy. Let's call him Orpheus

He's quite famous. Good at music

Okay, so there's a lot of stuff written about Orpheus, about how he was this great guy, great poet, amazing at the lyre

Right, but there's not that much about what he was actually like, you know what I mean?

Like, for example, like… I've seen a lot of pictures of him. Okay. A lot of paintings. There's hundreds, maybe thousands. And I shit you not, in every picture. In every picture… He's got his top off

Like every single one

And alright, he's got a nice body, but you know it's *every* picture

And you know, he was always playing his lyre

Like all the time, walking around, playing his lyre

Singing. Just walking around, through the forest, through the field, by the river, anywhere he wanted, any time of day, middle of the night, doesn't care. Are you getting this?

Okay, because the other thing I haven't told you, okay. The other thing I haven't mentioned is that Orpheus is the son of a king

His father is king

And you know who taught him to play the lyre?

God

Beat.

So you're imagining this? There's a guy, son of a king, a god as his music teacher, and he's walking around, top off, chest out, singing

And the thing is, in all the books, all the writings about Orpheus, they talk about how everyone was enchanted by him, his song was so beautiful, that everyone, and I mean everyone, people, animals, rivers, trees. They just loved him.

Okay, but what they don't say, what they don't tell you, is that his song was so loud, and so powerful, that they couldn't hear their own song

They couldn't hear themselves.

Silence.

Except… Sometimes… In the quiet hours, when they were alone, with themselves. Or with their children, or their lovers. Sometimes then, they could hear it. Their own songs. Their own language, in their own mouths. Their own voice.

It's just, outside, it was only Orpheus

Son of a king

Pupil of the gods

Deaf, but to himself

Pause.

So what happened to Orpheus?

Okay. So. He's walking around one day, singing his song and he comes across the Ciconian women.

And the Ciconian women, they're tired. They're so tired of Orpheus's song. Because Orpheus's song, has been playing in their ears since they could remember.

And one of the women, she spots him, and she says – to her friends, she says 'there he is, that motherfucker, with his fucking lyre again'

She said it in Greek

She says I've had enough of this. It's gone on too long and she picks up a stone and throws it at Orpheus's head.

Beat.

It hits him. It's a great shot. Only the stone, it doesn't hurt him. Just bounces off like a marshmallow. Cus the stone is so intoxicated by Orpheus's song, that its heart's not really in it. It just falls off. Lands at his feet.

So the Ciconian women, they get together, they stand up, together. They throw stones, and they throw sticks, they throw their arrows, and their swords, and that's when they hear it

We hear a song.

Low at first

Just one woman

We listen.

And after a while, another woman joins in

The song gets louder.

And then another

Louder still.

And another, and another, and another

Everyone singing.

Until, the whole crowd is singing and they're crying, and they've got their fists in the air

And they keep going, don't stop, and their stones become melodies, and their arrows become words, and they speak the language of their souls

With their voices raised, they tear this son of the gods limb from limb
They give the animals their rightful names,
The trees blossom, green and reds
The plants multiply
The rivers swell
And their song is so loud, it is so loud, and so beautiful, that the world wakes up
It wakes up from its drugged-up sleep and it listens

Pause.

But then the gods wake up too

And they collect the scattered limbs of their dead son

And they sink the women into the ground, and twist their raised
fists into the knotted branches of trees

They sink all of them, a billion trees, a million acres

But if you listen, if you really listen

In the silence of a forest

You can hear them

Their fists raised high

Still singing

Their song.

Pentheus and Bacchus

This story's a funny one.

Lighten the mood – you know? – because these things can get
a bit dark.

But this one, this one's about Pentheus, who is a king.

And we all love a king but this king is a bit of a stick-in-the-
mud.

One day, a prophet comes to him – this man called Tiresias –
and Tiresias tells the king all about a new god: Bacchus.

Harmless enough. But Pentheus finds out that the people of his
city have have started to worship this Bacchus.

They worship him more than they worship Pentheus.

Because Bacchus is generous.

Bacchus tells the people to drink and the people listen. Day and
night. Wine flowing. Music. Dancing. Orgies, sometimes, if you
know the right people.

But you see, Pentheus, he doesn't know any of the right people.

No orgies for Pentheus – he just doesn't get it. It's all too modern and scary for him so he tries to stop the people from worshipping Bacchus.

He even tries to get Bacchus arrested.

It doesn't work.

The people he sends to arrest Bacchus come back as devout followers!

And Pentheus is not happy: if you want a job done properly, do it yourself.

Now, everyone tells him not to, but Pentheus – stick-in-the-mud – decides he needs to take action.

And this is the funny bit: he sets out, alone, to arrest Bacchus. But instead of finding the god, he comes across a gathering of the god's followers.

Everyone is there: everyone who has told him to stay at home, including Pentheus's own family, they're all there and they all see Pentheus.

What happens next is Bacchus sends his followers into a frenzy.

Bacchus makes them think that Pentheus is a wild pig.

They hunt the wild pig.

Pentheus runs but his own mother grabs her son by the hand.

She rips it off.

Like wet paper.

Then she rips off the other.

Pentheus holds up the bloodied stubs as another woman – his own aunt – looks into her nephew's eyes and tears off his arm.

Someone else grabs his foot.

His calf.

His thigh.

Pentheus is screaming.

Someone reaches into his mouth, digs in her nails and pulls out his tongue.

He goes silent as dozens of hands grip his head and twist it off.

The segments of Pentheus are left scattered as the women go to the temple and pray.

To Bacchus.

–

Huh.

–

I told you it was a funny story.

Phaethon and Phoebus

Imagine you're the Sun

Are you imagining it?

You're very hot.

And quite bright.

Okay, now imagine that you fall in love with a woman. Her name is Clymene. And Clymene, you really love her. She's a great person. Not only is she your lover, but just sort of your friend, makes you laugh. Which is important to you, because it's quite lonely being the Sun. You've not really got many mates, no one wants to go near you, and most people won't even look at you.

But anyway, Clymene and you fall in love, she conceives a child, a boy. You call him Phaethon.

Now, things aren't straightforward, because they never are, are they, with love? And to make matters worse, you're the Sun, you're very busy. You work every day, and in the summer, it can be like, eighteen-hour shifts, it's very intense, which is all to say, you're not really around for much of the child's life

You're never around

Clymene isn't wild about this, she would prefer it if you were about a bit more but she does understand. You're the Sun for fuck's sake.

So anyway, the boy grows up. He grows big and he grows strong and he grows very handsome (he takes after you) and one day he turns to his mother and he says 'Mother, who's my father?'

And Clymene says, 'Your father is actually the Sun.' And Phaethon, though he's a lovely child, he's not the sharpest tool in the box

He's actually very stupid

He says to his mother 'I don't believe you'

And his mother, well… she's pretty hurt by this, understandably, she's spent her whole life, raising this child, single-handedly, day in day out, and here he is, questioning her.

She says to her son

'If you don't believe you can go'

'Go,' she says, 'off you go'

'Fuck off Phaethon, you ungrateful little shit'

'Ask him. Ask your father. Let him take a bit of responsibility for once'

And Phaethon is kind of stunned. He's never heard his mother speak like this. And he knows in his heart, he should just apologise. But the problem with Phaethon is that as well as being stupid he was also quite stubborn. So off he goes, to the Palace of the Sun.

The space transforms. Becomes the Sun Palace.

Now, the Palace of the Sun is very beautiful. It's very bright. Lots of gold. You might call it a bit 'showy'. But it's the Palace of the Sun, so what do you expect?

And in the middle of all this was Phoebus, the Sun. In human form.

Now Phoebus, looks at this fifteen-year-old boy, and he doesn't recognise him, to Phoebus he's just a kid. And so he says

'Boy. State your name and your purpose. What brings you here, to the Palace of the Sun?'

And Phaethon raises his voice. He's shitting it, but whilst he's definitely stupid, and he's also quite stubborn, the one thing he has got, is courage

And so he says 'My mother Clymene told me I'm your son. Is this true?'

And suddenly Phoebus looks at the boy. And his face softens. He sees, the outline of his own jaw, he sees, the brightness of his own eyes, he sees, his mother's smile, he sees this child he loves and he is overcome with joy

So Phoebus swoops down to pick up the child, but Phaethon, feeling the burn of his father's doubt says

'How can I trust you? You didn't even recognise me'

And Phoebus is not well practised at parenting, he doesn't know what to do. He loves this child – bit disappointing that he didn't recognise him – but still he really loves him. He tells him he's sorry. He says

'I want you to know. It's all for you.'

'This whole world, everything I'm doing, it's all for you'

But Phaethon, still not convinced, says to his father 'Prove it'

And Phoebus, looks at his son, flabbergasted, he says 'How can I prove it?'

But Phaethon just looks at him, unrelenting

So Phoebus say to him 'I'll grant you any wish. Anything you want. On this whole planet, as far as your eye can see, anything you want, you can have, let the gods bear witness

And Phaethon looks around, and he sees his father's golden chariot, and with his hand he points and says

'I'll take that.'

A shift.

Now, Phoebus was a big man. Sun God. He knew how to drive that steed, he knew how to hold fast through the high climbs, how to steer those horses through the ascent of the heavens, how to skirt the great seas, how to steer that chariot across the curvature of the globe, with reins safely in hand. He knew this as his life's work. He knew the perils of failure. As he knew his son would surely fail. And so he said to his son:

'Anything but the chariot'

'That chariot, it will be your death. Those horses will outrun you, and the fire of their wings will burn you, you take it now, you will surely die. And what's more… you'll set the world aflame'

But Phaethon was stupid,

and he was stubborn

'You swore it, with the gods as witness,' he said 'if you don't let me, then you break an oath. You swore I could have whatever I wished and what I wish, is to drive your chariot'

And so with a heavy heart. Phoebus handed him the reins.

The actors act out the next:

So Phaethon went

With ropes of gold

And a chariot of fire

And the wingèd steeds of power

He carried the Sun

The world at his feet

He climbed up through the sky, the reins tight in his hand

He chased away the moon

And scorched the heavens

He reached the highest point

His eyes wild

As he burst through the earth's atmosphere

To the stars in heaven

And from here, he could see everything. From this high he could see the whole world. From this high he could watch the clouds move, and the oceans swell, he could see the stretch of vast deserts and the snow-capped mountain peaks, from this high he could see the immense beauty this blue and brown and green planet, that we call home, he could see it hover, he could see it glow.

And for one moment everything was perfect. For one small moment it was just so...

But then the reins slipped.

And the first horses bolted.

And now Phaethon begins to fall

Down, down, through vast emptiness, the air sucked from his lungs, he falls, through the earth's atmosphere in his chariot of fire

And with this:

He scorches the land

He melts the ice caps

The oceans rise

The forests burn

The crops die out

The trees wither

The rivers run dry

The earth cracks

The people migrate

The water runs out

The fish die

The animals perish

The land is scorched with famine

And still Phaethon falls, his chariot ablaze, burning everything in his path

And Phoebus watches

His favourite son

as he sets fire to the world

And he thinks

Is this what I wanted

Is this what I was working for?

This child of mine, is this what I wanted

and the sky is full of smoke, and the oceans are empty, and the world is whimpering, it's screaming, it's scorched and burning and Phoebus thinks, as Jupiter strikes Phaethon from the sky with a bolt of thunder, he thinks

I did this

I did this

This was me

Philemon and Baucis

PHILEMON. At the moment, we are old.

We don't want for much and our days unfold in an unmistakable pattern.

BAUCIS. Sitting, eating, sleeping.

PHILEMON. And sometimes we have sex.

BAUCIS. If my back doesn't hurt.

PHILEMON. Which is a rarity. But it is how it's always been. And we hardly remember a time that was different.

–

BAUCIS. Except for one time.

PHILEMON. One time, yes, when two strangers arrived at our home.

Unwashed.

Desperate.

BAUCIS. Asking for food and shelter.

PHILEMON. Because they had knocked on the door of every house in the neighbourhood and were turned down by every house in the neighbourhood.

BAUCIS. But we let them in.

PHILEMON. We did. We laid a rug out. Mostly to stop the mud going everywhere.

BAUCIS. We coaxed a flame out of the hearth and set a stew on the boil.

PHILEMON. Cabbage, small knuckles of meat.

BAUCIS. Which was about all we had.

PHILEMON. It bubbled on the stove in a small copper pot.

BAUCIS. And when it was ready, the table was laid.

PHILEMON. And we sat.

> Awkward at first, but we couldn't help that, what do you say to a stranger?

> But we smiled at them, made small talk.

> And then we noticed how these strangers seemed a bit...

BAUCIS. Strange. Odd. You know. They kept nudging each other, they kept their faces hidden with their cloaks.

> I tried thinking nothing of it, I offered them wine.

PHILEMON. To relax things.

> And very quickly they finished the wine.

BAUCIS. Because they drank a lot, these strangers.

PHILEMON. A bit rude, if we're honest.

BAUCIS. And I think I went searching for more wine.

PHILEMON. Except there wasn't any.

BAUCIS. And we started panicking.

PHILEMON. Because to disappoint a guest in your own home is as shameful a thing as anything I can think of.

BAUCIS. And you were about to explain our lack of wine, weren't you?

PHILEMON. I was. All very nervous.

BAUCIS. But then a miracle occurred.

PHILEMON. As I stand here now.

BAUCIS. The wine welled up – didn't it?

> All by itself.

> It filled the bottle.

PHILEMON. And as we watched, we were transfixed.

BAUCIS. We looked at these strangers.

PHILEMON. Who seemed to be giggling now.

BAUCIS. We looked at each other.

PHILEMON. And we started to suspect something.

BAUCIS. Because they kept drinking, and the wine kept refilling, and these strangers' words kept slurring, their cloaks kept slipping until finally –

PHILEMON. We saw that they were gods!

BAUCIS. In our house. True as true can be.

PHILEMON. Swear on it. Jupiter and Mercury. Stood in front of us. Pissed.

BAUCIS. And they pointed at us.

PHILEMON. They did, they spoke.

BAUCIS. *COME WITH US. WE HAVE A PRESENT FOR YOU.*

PHILEMON. And I remember trying to think up an excuse.

BAUCIS. I remember not finding one.

PHILEMON. Because when the gods offer us humans a present, it usually isn't a present.

BAUCIS. You might have figured that out by now.

–

But there was nothing to be done. How could we say no?

PHILEMON. We followed them.

We followed them as they staggered up to the top of a mountain.

As they tripped up along the way.

BAUCIS. Their eyes red and bleak and cavernous.

PHILEMON. As they gestured out across the land, as they drawled on:

BAUCIS. *YOUR FELLOW HUMANS ARE CRUEL – THEY DESERVE PUNISHMENT.*

PHILEMON. As they smiled.

BAUCIS. *WE WILL DESTROY THEM.*

PHILEMON. As the land in front of us flooded.

In a flash.

Everything we knew – our home, our lives, our friends, our relatives, everything washed away… Except us.

BAUCIS. *FOR WE WILL GIVE YOU A REWARD.*

PHILEMON. With us, they offered a choice.

BAUCIS. *FOR YOUR KINDNESS, WE WILL GIVE YOU A PALACE: SERVANTS AND FOOD AND WINE, RICHES BEYOND BELIEF*

PHILEMON. Or…

BAUCIS. *WE CAN OFFER YOU A SINGLE WISH. SOMETHING YOU MUST BOTH EQUALLY DESIRE, BEYOND ANYTHING ELSE.*

–

PHILEMON. Except we weren't allowed to discuss it.

BAUCIS. We had to state the same wish

PHILEMON. at the same time

BAUCIS. using the same words…

–

PHILEMON. When we die	BAUCIS. When we die
Let our breath disappear	Let our breath disappear
at the same moment.	at the same moment.
So we may never see	So we may never see
the grave of the other.	the grave of the other.

–

BAUCIS. The gods smiled. They disappeared into the sky.

And now all we do is wait as our days fizzle out.

PHILEMON. Days which press down on our shoulders.

BAUCIS. Which tire out our bones and the ground wraps itself around our feet.

PHILEMON. We are sinking in, our breath is short.

BAUCIS. We feel some kind of darkness approach.

PHILEMON. And in this moment – we watch each other, we know what is happening – I see her sprout leaves.

BAUCIS. I see him sprout leaves.

PHILEMON. I see twigs twist out of her skin.

BAUCIS. Out of his skin – and before he says goodbye his lips are smothered in bark.

PHILEMON. –

BAUCIS. And the bark crawls across my skin.

As it does, I picture a thousand years: two trees – ancient – grown into the earth together – holding up the sky together.

And as the bark spreads further, I picture the thousand years after that, and a thousand after that, and it's

They transform into trees.

Procne and Philomela

1.

Procne and Philomela were sisters, both of them, daughters of Pandion

And Pandion was a good man. A good man, but a bad king. He lacked courage. It's somewhere around 8 AD and Athens is at war. The city is under siege

The soldiers have come and they've raped and they've pillaged and they've plundered and in the streets the people are starving, they're crying out, jewelled in the blood of their own relatives and many of them have lost all hope and into this walks Tereus

And Tereus is a king

He has money

And he brings his money and his soldiers and he defends the city, and because of this, Athens is saved, the soldiers leave. The people rejoice

Only…

Only, that's not the whole story, because Tereus, he's not a good man, he says to Pandion

'I saved your city. Now you must pay me'

And Pandion. Is scared. His city has been pillaged, his crops burned, his people slaughtered, he has nothing to offer, but his life and he doesn't want to do that because of his daughters. Procne and Philomela.

He turns to Tereus and he asks him 'What is it you want from me?' And Tereus, he doesn't flinch, he looks back at Pandion, looks him straight in the eye and he says

'I want your daughters'

Beat.

So Pandion is terrified. Like we said, he lacks courage. He looks at his daughters, both of whom are young still, he looks at them, and he says 'Take Procne.'

The eldest

There is a wedding

Huge

Tables bedecked in gold, overflowing with wine, the finest meats, fresh fruit

Only... No one came

And this, bride, still a child really, in her virginal white silk was stood alone and ghostlike in the middle of the banquet.

Juno wasn't there. Nor Hymen, not one of the Graces, no one, except the Furies, who rose up from the plundered city, snatching brands from the burning dead and wielding them as torches to light the wedding

Poor Procne. Poor girl, who lay silent, eyes shut, teeth clenched, swallowed sobs as her groom fucked her in their nuptial quarters

Because you couldn't call it rape

He'd married her. And back then you couldn't call it rape to force a woman if you'd married her

An owl flew through the black sky, and sat, all night over the bridal suite, until, as morning dawned, Procne, looked over at her husband,

and she looked at herself

Her own eyes in the mirror

And an ache as big as an ocean swelled up inside her chest, as she thought about her new life, and all the days and days and days of it, and she felt in her stomach the seed of a child

A boy

She felt it growing

2.

Time passes, years. Procne has a child, a boy, Itys. He's a sweet boy. It's not his fault, but sometimes when she looks at him, she sees the torches of funeral pyres in his eyes, or hears the call of a death owl in his voice

She gets on with it. All the days and days and days of it

When her father writes to her, she tells him she's fine. She says 'I love it here, it's great'

And she does this because she knows if she told the truth, her truth, she would get

Silence.

So she keeps her mouth shut, keeps silent. And she puts on make-up, and plaits her hair, and she kisses her child as she puts him to bed, and sometimes, she catches the eye of a guard, and she knows, he's seen the mark on her shoulder, or he's heard, the whimpers of a woman, who is swallowing her pain, and sometimes she says

'Did you see that?' And they say

Silence.

And once she said 'Will you help me?' And they said

Silence.

And so she remains, in the palace of silence, lit up with the flames of the burned dead, and she lives

This silence

All the days of it

Until one day

When she's tying her hair, she catches herself in the glassy reflection of a still lake, and she remembers, the snatch of her sister's smile, and she's suddenly filled with a longing so deep, so profound, she can't bear it, she goes to Tereus, she says

'I need to see my sister. It's been too long. I need to see her, if I don't see her, I might drown, in an ocean of my own longing. Will you bring her to me? Across the wide sea, will you bring her. I need to see her. Or I'll die.' She says 'A thousand times I'll die' And so Tereus goes, in a boat, across the ocean.

To Athens

3.

Now when Tereus arrives in Athens, and he sees Philomela, she looks different to him. She seems grown, beautiful, Tereus wants her.

But the thing about Philomela, though she's only fifteen. She's smart, she senses something in Tereus, and she thinks about all those letters, from Procne, and she remembers, water-stained edges, smeared ink, and though her father doesn't want Philomela to leave, she insists, she has an instinct. She needs to see Procne. And so she goes, with Tereus, across the violent sea

Tereus, he takes Philomela to a hut

Deep in the forest, and there he rapes her. We can call it rape because she's not his wife. He forces her, it's brutal, she screams, she isn't silent, It lasts a long time. And when Tereus is done, and he stands there breathless and gulping, looking at the child before him

Tereus is ashamed

He's so ashamed

To meet himself, in his true form, that he can't bear it, and so he takes his knife and he cuts out her tongue

PHILOMELA *spits out her bloodied tongue.*

and when Tereus gets to the palace, and Procne asks him where her sister is, he replies 'She died. At sea. A tragedy' and Procne weeps for her dead sister, she walls herself in the palace of silence. Until at last she resigns herself to it

This life

This child

This fate

4.

Philomela is entrusted to the care of a nobleman. She's given a maid. Now the nobleman knows what has happened to Philomela, he knows exactly what's gone on. But he doesn't want to say anything, he thinks it's not his business

He gives Philomela a change of clothes and a cloth to clean herself, he brushes it under the carpet

For a year she weaves. Every day she weaves. A huge tapestry. She barely sleeps, because though Tereus cut out her tongue, he didn't extinguish her flame. She makes quick work, furious work, till after a year, she has finished

And this tapestry, it looks like hell

It rages, with all the details, everything Philomela has lived through. She takes this tapestry to her maid, and when she unfolds it, this maid – she knows what to do

Now a silence has taken hold of the whole palace. No one speaks there any longer, not even the child, who was conceived of terrible silence, and for whom silence is the only language he knows. Into this comes Philomela's maid, carrying her weave and, upon receiving it, Procne cries out. A hollowed-out, animal cry, that stirs something deep within her

Immediately Procne heads to the forest, and on seeing Philomela, now sixteen, the same age as she, when she married Tereus, she gets on her knees and she cries, bitter tears, and she swears to avenge her sister. She swears that she will.

A pause.

Can I ask you lot a question?

Have you ever witnessed something. Something bad. Something, like unjust. You know? Like you've ever been witness to something, or maybe not actual witness, but you've known something was going on, and you knew and you knew and you knew and you did nothing?

Like I remember being in a play, this play from years ago, it was my first job, and the director was a real arsehole, actually, he was a real, you know, just total narcissist. And he clearly fancied one of the actors, and he would give her so much shit. One time we'd gone out after rehearsals, and he'd got so drunk that he was just all over her, I saw them in the corner of this bar we were in, and it was like he'd pinned her, he was all over her, pissed, sweating, his fucking hands all over her legs

And later I'd seen her coming out the toilets and all her make-up had run, you could tell she'd been crying, she looked at me, this look, that was just like…

I don't know why I'm telling you this.

I still think about it

I still think about it

The actor looks at PHILOMELA*'s bloodied mouth.*

Procne and Philomela devise a plan, what they do is this

They go to the tender boy, Itys, not yet eight years of age, they stroke his hair and take him by the hand to the most silent of all the silent rooms in the palace of silence: the room of his conception. And there, while the child cries out to her, Procne drives a sword through his chest. As he reaches his arms toward her, she cuts him down. She drives a spear through his stomach and neck, she hacks at his body in terrible bloody silence, and when the butchery is over, and the deed is done, she boils him in a pot and she feeds him to his father.

Someone screams.

When Tereus turning from his bloodstained feast sees Procne, and asks calmly where the child is, Procne gestures to his bowl. Philomela now revealed, stands bloody, and silent, *still* silent in the doorway, and Tereus, finally understanding the end of the course he set in action, burns from the inside

And the sisters transform.

PROCNE *reaches inside her mouth, and she pulls from it two birds – a swallow and a nightingale.*

They go, two birds, shedding their mortal coil.

The birds fly.

And Tereus, he becomes a crow and he chases after them, in haste

Procne becomes a swallow and Philomela, she becomes a nightingale. And the nightingale's song is still thought to be the most beautiful. Have you ever heard it? Have you ever?

But you know, it's not the female that sings

It's not Philomela

That's what they don't tell you

And I only know this story, because I overheard it, in a bar, two friends, in hushed tones

Because those guards they never said a word. Not to anyone who mattered. And that nobleman, nor did he. And the palace of silence, it remained in silence.

The boiled limbs of a dead child stewed on the kitchen table

Because some silences, they last forever.

www.nickhernbooks.co.uk

facebook.com/nickhernbooks

twitter.com/nickhernbooks